niace · lifelines in adult learning

3

Managing community projects for change

Jan Eldred

Published by the National Institute of
Adult Continuing Education (England and Wales)

21 De Montfort Street
Leicester LE1 7GE
Company registration no. 2603322
Charity registration no. 1002775

First published 2002

The *NIACE lifelines in adult learning series* is supported by the Adult
and Community Learning Fund. ACLF is funded by the Department
for Education and Skills and managed in partnership by NIACE and
the Basic Skills Agency to develop widening participation in adult learning.

promoting adult learning

NIACE has a broad remit to promote lifelong learning
opportunities for adults. NIACE works to develop
increased participation in education and training,
particularly for those who do not have easy access
because of barriers of class, gender, age, race,
language and culture, learning difficulties and
disabilities, or insufficient financial resources.

www.niace.org.uk

Cataloguing in Publication Data
A CIP record of this title is available from the British Library

Designed and typeset by Boldface
Printed in Great Britain by Russell Press, Nottingham

ISBN 1 86201 141 9

Contents

Note to the reader:

Inspirations: refer to case studies and examples of good practice.
Glossary: the meanings of the words <u>underlined in the text</u> can be found in the glossary on pages 39 and 40.

1 Why projects?

"We want more mainstream funding"

Many people argue that we should simply increase the mainstream funding for adult learning rather than offer more short-term project funding. Indeed, there are valid arguments to be made to support such claims. However, the need for project funding is unlikely to disappear and we should encourage its growth, in addition to continuing to make the case for increasing funding to sustain and develop mainstream activities.

Projects are a valuable and essential part of adult learning activities because they:

- offer opportunities to develop and test new ideas.
- allow us to experiment and take risks.
- can target resources, good practice and ideas in particular geographical areas or for specific groups of people.
- provide opportunities for action research where ideas, processes and outcomes can be compared, and where results, trends and patterns can be identified and disseminated to inform future practices.
- create frameworks for developing and disseminating interesting and good practice.
- allow rapid responses to new or crisis situations such as the impact of foot-and-mouth disease, redundancies or refugees.
- encourage new and different players such as Trusts and Foundations to contribute to adult learning, in a way which enhances their aims but enables them to add to the widening of participation, for example through a focus on children, housing or disability.
- establish the base upon which future mainstream funding can build by demonstrating what works, prior to mainstream commitment.
- help funders and providers to set short-term aims and objectives to achieve particular goals – perhaps to address inequalities or gaps in practices or

provision, for example the Quality Initiative for Inclusion.
* help new providers and practitioners to demonstrate and build their capacity to deliver good quality learning opportunities.

To project means to look forward. Projects can carry forward inspiration, ideas and creative thinking into their realisation, in ways which have the capacity to change people and situations.

Why projects matter

"The SKILL project has been a major impetus in the setting up of the Community Learning Centre. This is the only daytime provision in the town that offers a range of learning opportunities. It will, hopefully, provide a model for centres in other rural market towns."
(The SKILL project,
C G Partnership)

"The strength of the project continues to lie in its distinctive non-traditional approach to working with young people as creative individuals. The programme combines collaborative learning with supported opportunities for personal originality. The aim is to work in response to the actual interests of learners, within a positive context for creative and cultural education."
(Second Wave Open Learning Programme)

"The project has achieved far more than was originally anticipated in relation to student numbers, mainly due to the project's outreach work... We have achieved sustainability for some courses... the partnership will ensure provision of free reminiscence sessions for older people at the museum... A number of residential care venues are buying-in the project's range of activities. Other group activities have been taken over by Adult Education... other groups have been advised about funding opportunities and are running their own classes. We are now working with the LSC... to extend the training and activities offer by the project."
(The Living Memory Project, Norfolk Adult Education Service)

2 Adult learning projects

Projects can be described in different ways, according to the purposes they serve:

- targeted, developmental activities which are focused on a particular geographical area, target group or theme.
- demonstration activities, designed to change provision, practices and people by filling an identified gap or adding to existing provision.
- catalysts which attempt to redress imbalances and inequalities.
- opportunities to test or prove new and different ways of working.

Projects have characteristics in common, regardless of their focus, context or duration. They are usually:

- carried out over a limited period of time.
- designed in response to some form of needs analysis.
- planned to achieve stated aims and objectives.
- focused on planned outcomes but open to identifying unplanned or additional outcomes.
- resourced in a targeted way to achieve the aims, objectives and outcomes.
- required to prepare budgets, keep accounts and produce reports.
- obliged to monitor and evaluate their activities in order to gain insight about how the project can develop and improve.
- asked to disseminate the results of the work.

Quality assurance mechanisms underpin the delivery of projects. These include:

- supporting project staff.
- supporting project participants.
- supporting equality of opportunity in relation to publicity, reaching and recruiting participants, teaching materials.
- operating rigorous health and safety systems which ensure the safety of staff and participants in all premises and outreach situations.
- monitoring, review and evaluation strategies.
- reporting and dissemination mechanisms.

The parameters set out in the project proposal, and agreed by the funders, form the framework for managing a project.

Targeting particular areas and groups

In order to attract women from large, peripheral housing estates, who experienced social isolation, the North Hull Women's Centre ran a project which provided small steps from informal learning, tasters, and short courses through to accredited opportunities. All the activities were negotiated with the women who were supported into tuition through outreach, guidance and counselling, childcare and personal support. The women were supported into running the centre and provision so that their learning was not confined to the planned programmes and activities but included experiencing new roles and responsibilities.

(The Willow Project, Kingston Upon Hull)

Filling a gap in provision

First Base Walsall, which provides support for young homeless people and workers, identified that with appropriate guidance and support their clients could be encouraged into learning opportunities on-site. This added to the range of services they could offer by guiding the young people into tailored, fun activities leading into skill-based programmes which would enhance their employment prospects. The project experimented with what seemed to work best, built the capacity of the organisation and gave it the opportunity to gain accredited status as an Information and Guidance provider.

INSPIRATIONS

Inequalities and imbalances

Keighley Healthy Living Network identified that many people from Black and Minority Ethnic groups were not accessing health- related services and activities, especially in relation to mental ill-health. They developed a project which aimed to involve women in community activities which valued their cultural diversity but tackled the issues of stress and mental ill-health. In this way they opened up opportunities to people who were unequally represented in services which are designed for the whole community.

Testing new and different ways of working

Fircroft College used the development of a play to address issues associated with access to learning for people marginalised by their health concerns. By contacting non-participants, via health agencies, a community-based drama was created around the issues and barriers they identified and then performed to a wide range of audiences of practitioners, providers and professionals. In this way, potential learners were involved in raising awareness and helping to change perceptions and practice for the future, whilst being supported into learning themselves.
(The Play's the Thing project)

3 Why project management is important

In an adult learning environment, where bidding for project funding is part of daily life for the majority of providers, good practice in project management is one of the keys to success, not only in realising the project but also in bidding for the next funding opportunity. It is sometimes the case that large institutions are involved in managing scores of different funding streams, and many of these are for project work. Whether for large, experienced providers, or small, new ones, good project management develops the capacity of the organisation, builds the confidence of their funders, and promotes a virtuous cycle towards future success.

The plethora of funding sources is unlikely to diminish, so those who are best able to manage their projects are likely to be the winners. The challenges facing larger organisations include the temptation to retain funds, excessively, to support central services, as well as how effectively to influence future planning and embed

Hammersmith & Fulham Action for Disability: A student learning to touch-type

RICHARD OLIVIER

projects in their wider services. Smaller organisations need to ensure that they have staff, systems and procedures in place to support their project and to ensure that project initiatives do not distract them from their mission or distort the services they offer. Good project management, therefore, is an issue for all providers of adult learning.

The audit culture has an important influence. If it is not to become a headache, the introduction of sound, uncomplicated systems can help project providers to have stress-free audits. The balance between the need for accountability and engagement in a bureaucratic nightmare is likely to be maintained with good project management.

Project management helps to ensure that good ideas are well and truly implemented. The creative ideas and processes, which often motivate, drive and reward projects, can be lost if management issues dominate or drain. Good management works to ensure systems and procedures are in place to deal with eventualities and challenges, allowing more creative dimensions to develop. Good project management supports rather than controls the activities which shape and energise the project.

The aims and objectives of a project are likely to be realised if the project is managed from the outset with a view to their achievement.

The key movers and shakers of project work are usually the project staff. They need to be managed sensitively and offered clear management, good communication strategies, a flexible approach – which recognises that community project work is not a regular 9-to-5 job – and the opportunity to develop their skills and knowledge in the job. Their health and safety should also be considered in new environments and activities.

RICHARD OLIVIER

Merseyside Heritage Project, Liverpool: Repairing a hatch aboard the Brigantine ZEBU

4 OK! You got the money – the project process

Projects are characterised by processes which follow similar patterns, regardless of their size or duration. These include:

- project design and work-plans
- partnership planning
- delivery
- monitoring, review and evaluation
- celebrations
- moving on – exit strategies
- conclusions and final reports.

The processes create a clear framework for those who plan, organise and deliver the project. They attempt to establish accountability to participants, providers and sponsors. They also recognise that projects move in and out of communities. If people are aware of the processes and parameters, integrity about the method of working can be established.

Project models can feed into a cycle of development which leads a project, or some strands of it, into mainstream funding sources. Good processes also help projects to strengthen their position when applying for further projects. By identifying ideas, showing an understanding of the under-pinning concepts, and demonstrating their competence in implementing them as well as presenting evidence of the outcomes, projects prepare groups and organisations for future work.

5 Key project roles and responsibilities

Project manager:

- appoints the project co-ordinator
- clarifies roles and responsibilities of the co-ordinator and other project staff
- clarifies communications, meetings and relationships with the management group and steering group
- supports the co-ordinator.

Project co-ordinator:

- appoints members of the project team
- develops the work-plan with the team
- develops action plans with the team
- oversees and manages the work of the team to deliver the planned outcomes
- regularly reviews with individuals and the team
- supports the team
- keeps a diary of project activity
- reports to the manager, management group and steering group
- contributes to evaluation strategies
- drafts the final report with the team and manager.

Project staff:

- deliver the day-to-day activities of the project
- review regularly with participants
- support participants
- report to the team and co-ordinator
- attend team meetings and contribute to monitoring and evaluation strategies.

Management group:

- receives reports from the co-ordinator and manager
- supports new or modified action in the light of reports
- contributes to the monitoring and evaluation strategies
- monitors that the project is achieving its outcomes and makes recommendations for any amendments
- supports the co-ordinator and manager.

Steering group:

- receives reports from the co-ordinator and manager
- contributes to the monitoring and evaluation
- assists with dissemination of outcomes
- keeps the wider community informed of progress and developments.

CEDAR/North Tyneside, East Howden Community Centre, Newcastle: Jan Leslie talking with Marcus Beaumont, project co-ordinator

RICHARD OLIVIER

6 Project design and work-plans

The project is shaped by the proposal which was outlined in the application process and agreed by the funders. Invariably there are details which need to be worked on before delivery can be implemented. The aims, objectives and outcomes agreed, as well as the funding, become the controls for the design of the project. A detailed examination of the proposal, extracting key activities, partners, targets and milestones, all help to clarify what planning needs to be undertaken. It is vital to bear in mind what is feasible when designing the project: ideas and implementation are not always the same. Using the SMART guidance can be helpful.

S	=	Specific
M	=	Measurable
A	=	Achievable
R	=	Relevant
T	=	Time-bound

Asking yourself and colleagues whether the goals and targets are SMART is a good test of whether your ideas are going to deliver the outcomes you seek.

Keeping in touch with the funders and the guidance they offer is another important design feature. In planning the detail, their requirements must be considered. This includes when delivery can begin and end, when funding can be drawn, when reports and accounts must be submitted, what the funding can pay for (some funds are very particular about capital and revenue allocations) and what monitoring and evaluation must be carried out.

Drafting a work-plan can help in creating a structure for the project by setting out the timetable for activities to be initiated, delivered, reviewed and reported upon. It also provides a vehicle for everyone involved in the project to share the practicalities of realising the project vision. Project partners should be included in this process.

Drafting a work-plan

Meet as a project team to discuss the work-plan and agree who will write it. The whole team should contribute to the plan but only one person needs to draft it.

Share the plan with the team before finalising it.

Start with the objectives of the project:

- What activities need to be undertaken?
- Who will be responsible for carrying them out?
- When will the activities be conducted?
- What resources are needed?

Think about the timescale of the project, the sequence of activities, the costs involved at each stage and whether the people have the skills, support and time needed to complete the activities successfully. Staff training and development may need to be included in the plan as well as a planning and start-up phase.

Include promotional events, day-to-day activities, review meetings, management, partnership and steering group meetings, monitoring stages, evaluation activities, dissemination events, reporting and accounting dates in the work-plan.

Plans can be written in a framework with headings such as:

- Date
- Planned activity
- Who involved
- Resources needed
- Planned outcome
- Review comments

They can also include phases such as:

- Planning
- Start-up
- Delivery
- Disseminating and celebrating

Use the work-plan to monitor the work, to recognise achievements along the way and to add or amend the activities to meet the planned outcomes.

If the work-plan is a shared document, monitoring, problem-solving and development of the project should involve all the key players.

Norfolk County Council: Reminiscence and Learning project: Valentine Barker Court sheltered housing

7
Partnership planning

Partners are often identified in project proposals. Some bidding processes require partnerships to be included in the projects they support. Ideally, partners will have been closely involved in drafting the initial ideas but occasionally they are mentioned in the hope that, if the funding is granted, they will subsequently get involved. Once approval to run the project has been given, all the partners mentioned should be contacted. In order to plan delivery, different partners need to be involved in different ways. It may be helpful to see some people as partners but others as allies or part of the project network.

Partners can be described as the people who have a shared interest in the process and outcomes of the project. Partners put something in and expect something out of the project. They are committed to the success of the whole project, not just part of it, and usually commit funds, staff, resources or time to

Proper Job Theatre Co/Above & Beyond Group, Lawrence Bailey Theatre, Huddersfield

RICHARD OLIVIER

INSPIRATIONS

UK Youth and the WEA

The UK Youth organisation identified that work with young, single mothers was needed in some large housing estates and so partnered the Workers' Educational Association (WEA) to work in two geographical areas, develop a programme with the young women, pilot the work and gain accredited status. Both organisations committed time, staff, experience, expertise and resources to achieve the project aim.

The WEA had experience of working in community settings, responding to identified needs, and UK Youth had experience of working with younger people and outreach to involve and engage them in activities. The interests and skills of both organisations were complementary and worked towards a common goal.

Example of allies/networks in a partnership project

A partnership between the Adult Education Service and the Early Years Partnership in Scunthorpe resulted in a project to support parents involved in Homestart into learning opportunities. Their allies included the local church which provided a community base. The local IAG service offered their support, and the networks of the three primary partners meant that individual participant needs were addressed using social service and adult education service links. In this example, the partnership was able to draw on allies who helped them realise their overall aim. (Broadening Horizons Project, Scunthorpe)

that end. This can be a new commitment or a diversion of existing resources to further the goals of the project. The commitment can be in cash or in kind. Partners can be internal to a large organisation, such as links across departments or sections, or external, across agencies and organisations. These partners need to be closely involved in drafting the work-plan and should be in constant contact with the project via the steering or management group.

Allies or network colleagues may be brought into the project at different stages or contribute skills or resources from time to time for a specific purpose. They may offer the use of a venue or equipment, refer people to the project or offer their services such as childcare or Information, Advice and Guidance (IAG). This involvement in the project may be offered as part of their ongoing work or purchased by the project, as and when needed.

Making partnerships work

Many projects set out with good intentions to work with other organisations and networks but find that, along the way, they are let down or become disillusioned by an apparent lack of commitment from others. There are some strategies which can be adopted to help such situations:

- be clear about who are partners and who are allies, associates or networks.
- limit the partnership to those people who are closely committed to working towards the project aim and have something to give and gain from it.
- gain the commitment of all partners and allies in writing, including the lead organisation or department, indicating what each will contribute and be responsible for.
- form a management group to guide the project. Membership should be drawn from the main partners and the key project workers. A critical friend from another organisation – who has an interest in the project outcomes – could also be included in this group, to offer perspective and help in the review of the operation of the project. This group is more likely to be a decision-making group than a steering group.
- form a steering group which draws representation from all the groups, agencies and organisations who have an interest in the project and its outcomes. This can help in keeping people on board. It can also keep the wider networks informed and involved and help embed the project in a broader context. Including representatives from organisations which might be interested in the project outcomes and implications once it is over can be a helpful strategy in sustaining work after the project is over.

- be clear about line management of the project on a day-to-day basis and ensure that communication is established with and from the management and steering groups.
- agree communication strategies such as reporting responsibilities and dissemination strategies. For example, who will draft agendas and write notes of meetings, and who will distribute the notes?
- tackle any discomfort in the partnership speedily but with sensitivity.

LEAP Project/Bristol Community Education Shop: Courses relating to employment issues are run at the Employment Shop

RICHARD OLIVIER

INSPIRATIONS

Action Disability

"The project management and structures and processes were effective because of the following factors:

- simplicity – simple management structures were maintained and allowed for a 'hands-on' approach.
- strong links and understanding of the local community and target group.
- a proven history in this field which attracted partners.
- an accessible resource centre.
- the development of links with partners who are committed to the aims and objectives of the project.

On the whole the project's experience of management and partnership has been a positive one. The organisation has strong links in the area it serves and is well known for its experience of working with the project target group. The project is a good example of how local networks can close gaps in provision. As a result of the project we have been approached by a number of providers to develop partnerships for future working." (Kensington and Chelsea Lifelong Learning Project)

8 Delivering the project

Once the partnerships and work-plans are agreed the delivery of the project can begin. The stages of delivery will be recorded in the work-plan from which small groups or individuals can create their own action plans.

Action plans

Action plans provide tools for individuals to achieve developmental goals toward an overall project aim. For example, a project which aims to discover what learning interests may lie within a community needs a work-plan designed to take the steps to achieve the aim. The individuals involved – such as the co-ordinator, the field workers, the guidance workers and the managers – all need their own action plans which ensure that they work towards achieving their own contributions to the project. Each must be clear about who is their line manager so that day-to-day issues can be addressed quickly and the plan can be reviewed jointly on a regular basis and modified in the light of progress.

Example of action plan format

Action Plan

Name:

Activity/project title:

Date	Activity (What do?)	Who/What resources needed?	Planned outcome	By when?	Review/ completion comments

Project diary

Another useful tool is a project diary. Such a diary is helpful, especially for project co-ordinators, in which key milestones for the project, including dates for steering and management meetings and reporting and accounting dates, can be recorded. This record informs future activity and planning. The diary also records activity and notes reflections and feedback which can then inform reports or meetings with line managers, management groups or steering groups. Reflective practice is thus built into the project in a simple, practical and informative way.

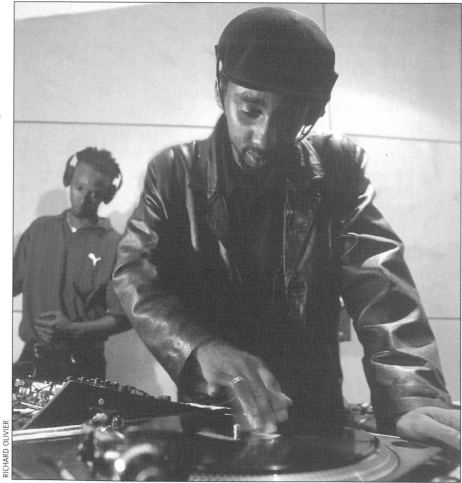

RICHARD OLIVIER

In the studio: Beat Dis Arts

9 Monitoring, review and evaluation

Strategies for <u>monitoring</u>, <u>review</u> and <u>evaluation</u> need to be established from the beginning of the project and incorporated into the work-plan. They may have been described in the project proposal which should form the basis of the approaches to be used in the project.

Monitoring means checking that activities, goals and outcomes (such as staff appointments, events, meetings, reports, numbers of participants) are taking place as planned. A regular review of the work-plan ensures that the project is progressing as planned. It is usually the responsibility of the project co-ordinator to report to the management group, using the information gained from monitoring. Where deviations from the plan are noted, these should be assessed and analysed, in order to understand the differences. Amendments and additions can then be made, in consultation with line managers, to guide the work towards the overall goals.

Financial monitoring is a vital part of the process. Budgets should be drafted, in line with the guidance given by the project sponsor. The responsibilities for coding and recording expenditure should be clearly allocated at the outset. Monitoring expenditure against the budget should be held regularly and reported to both project managers and the management group. Claiming of funds should be conducted within the sponsor's guidelines and monitoring reports should usefully coincide with the claim dates. These milestones should be recorded on the work-plan.

Reports and meeting notes are ways of keeping all the parties informed about the progress of the project. Whilst project workers often spend long hours preparing reports they are most effective if they follow agreed headings. A good format will include the following but should also follow the guidance of the management committee.

Report headings:

* What has been achieved from the work-plan
* The participants, target numbers, who they are, any feedback
* What is proving successful
* What is proving challenging
* The partnership
* Progress and learning gains

- Quality assurance
- Equal opportunities
- Financial report
- Next stage of development

Agreeing the format for meeting notes is also a useful tool to ensure efficient ways of recording meetings and the action points arising. The following is a possible outline:

Meeting notes format

People present:

Apologies:

Agenda items:
1. Notes of last meeting
2. Matters arising
3. Agenda item
4. Agenda item
5. Agenda item
6. Any other business
7. Date of next meeting

Item No.	Discussion points	Action: What? Who? When?

Review is the process of reflecting on, or looking back at, activities, events and stages of development, in order to discover what people think and feel. Review provides the opportunity to ask such questions as, "How was it for you?", "What was good and what not so good?", "What have you learned?" and "What could we do differently?" Reviews should be held for all the people involved in the project and at different stages along the way. They can be held on a one-to-one basis or in groups. Participants, practitioners, providers, management and steering groups should review what they do with a view to changing and adapting their practices, as the project develops. Reviews should be held during any one of the strands of activity which contribute to the project as well as at the end of the project. Reviews are either formative (shaping or forming) or summative (summarising, at the end). Reviews, which help to identify progression routes and support participants or staff into activities after the project has ended, are particularly important.

Reviews should be recorded so that they can be shared. This can be as notes in a diary, meeting notes or on an action plan. They can be private reflections using art as a vehicle to express thoughts, feelings and ideas which are then shared with others. Drama, music, poetry and creative writing give opportunities for individuals and groups to express what they experience from being involved in the project. Reviews can be discussions or comments recorded on flipcharts, graffiti boards, audio tape, videos or on photographs. Information from reviews feed into the wider process of evaluation of the project.

Evaluation is concerned with asking broader questions about whether the aims and objectives of the project are being met and what difference is being made. Is the project achieving what it set out to do, in the way it was hoped and planned? Is it making a difference to participants, practitioners, providers and the partners? How is the difference being identified, measured or recorded? Is it having an impact on the community it seeks to serve? Are there any unplanned outcomes, spin-offs, benefits (or otherwise) being observed, identified or reported? What seems to work best and why? What seems to be less effective and why?

The data from reviews should be gathered regularly and presented to the management and steering groups who should be asking the evaluative questions, along with project staff and managers. The evaluation should inform the on-going development of the project and make recommendations at the end of its work. These recommendations will inform future work and new projects.

Some projects appoint a colleague or an external agency to evaluate the work from the outset. The evaluator works alongside all the strands of activity and all the people involved and captures their responses. The insights and information are reported back to the steering group which can then identify what works and what should change.

The evaluation should be regarded as one of the most important aspects of the project because this process identifies what is effective in achieving the aims of the project. It is also the instrument which is used to make recommendations about changes in practices. Evaluation is the mechanism which can identify what everyone has learned as a result of being involved in the project. It demonstrates the value of particular activities, approaches and methodologies. It is also a way of identifying future project activity and sharing good practice. Evaluation is the way in which projects can demonstrate to everyone, including the sponsoring organisation, that their work has made a difference.

Disseminating the outcomes of evaluation can be imaginative and creative, such as using arts-based activities, photographs, exhibitions, dance and drama, sculpture, video and audio presentations, musical presentations, poetry and prose as well as reports, statistics and graphics.

Local Education Access Project

LEAP in Bristol used a wide range of methods to obtain monitoring information and improve the services they offered: "The usual monitoring procedures have been observed: tutor observations, evaluations by course participants, course steering meetings once a term and internal moderations. In addition, a LEAP get-together day was organised to bring together participants from different courses to discuss their experiences and to help the project learn about how to improve what it does. It also brought together tutors and participants and steering group members (for an informal lunch) in an effort to increase a sense of "LEAP" identity and belonging for participants, staff, tutors and other interested partners. The plan is to repeat this format...while adding an extra dimension of talks from local Access to HE providers to encourage participants to progress." (LEAP project report)

The Bridge Project

The Bridge Project in Tyne and Wear recognised that monitoring and evaluation had to be carried out by everyone concerned with the work: "Via a range of informal and formal mechanisms our learners evaluate the provision and have a say in what goes on in the centre and in the local community. Our courses are set up as a response to the needs that learners have identified and the curriculum, content and delivery methods are changed to suit learners' needs. Women have ownership of the project and are enjoying their learning experiences. The Bridge manager, the Board of Directors, the Consultancy and Advisory Group, the Partner Review Group and the co-ordinator and her staff team all play a part in monitoring and evaluating the project and ensuring that all the objectives in the Action Plan are being met." (project report)

INSPIRATIONS

Northallerton Wheels Project

Slightly more informal but nonetheless effective review processes were carried out by the Northallerton Wheels Project: "Methods for monitoring the progress of the individuals were a variety of base-line self-assessments, 6-month self-review and final self-review as well as chat-back forms, scoring their thoughts and achievements on a sessional review, and observational reports by the youth workers." (project report)

PROMIS Theatre project, Sheffield: Dancer Phil Destcroix leads a warm-up exercise

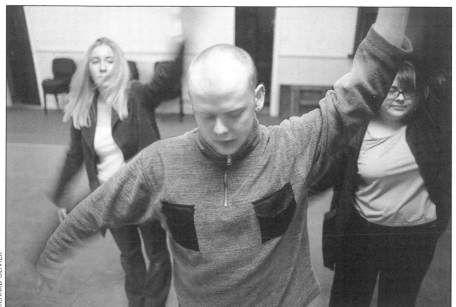

RICHARD OLIVIER

10 Celebration

Celebrating the work of the project can mark achievements of many kinds, including group and individual achievements as well as launches of new stages or phases of development. Celebrations help to raise the profile of the work, inform wider audiences about processes and outcomes, help to endorse the efforts of project staff and, most importantly, put the learners or participants in the spotlight. The celebration is a public acknowledgement of hard work and offers encouragement to individuals and groups. It can also help in the sustainability plans by informing those who might be interested in the continuing work of the project and about its successes.

Invitations to celebrations need to be carefully considered and include sponsors, steering and management groups, staff, community representatives, statutory services representatives and, of course, the participants. Participants' families should also be invited, to endorse the importance of the milestone in the learning journey, help support learners and even encourage others on board!

Projects use all kinds of ways to celebrate their work. Exhibitions, displays, performances, seminars, conferences, awards events, days out, trips on rivers and canals, residential events and demonstrations of skills developed are fairly high-profile activities which demand a great deal of planning and organisation. Publishing letters, poetry or prose, newsletters and photographs can also be effective ways of celebrating some of the outcomes of the project.

Celebrations are also opportunities for disseminating some of the project outcomes. This does not have to be in the form of a weighty report but can be small leaflets which detail some of the activities, photographs which show what has been done, videos and tapes, learner graffiti and feedback boards. Participants who tell their own stories about their involvement in the project can be a powerful way of demonstrating what a difference the project has made to them.

Most importantly, invite the press, radio and television to promote or attend your event. Include the local paper and local radio but don't forget that regional television is also often interested in community activities.

"You must celebrate with the group, for the group as well as the individuals in it."
(ACLF project focus group, Leicester)

"Present awards, not just at the end of the project but at different stages of the programme, to mark progress and small achievements, both planned and unexpected. Marking this kind of achievement means you can also take time to decide on the next steps. So, achievement is celebrated and also helps in identifying further steps towards progress."
(ACLF project focus group, London)

"Get learners to organise celebration events, displays and exhibitions as part of their learning."
(ACLF project focus group, Manchester)

11 Exit planning

Many sponsors of projects request information about exit plans at the point of application for funding. It is difficult to identify how a project which has not yet begun will end and what opportunities will be put in place for further development. However, it is vital to consider questions of <u>sustainability</u> and continuity from the outset. The reasons for this are because:

- everyone involved in the project should know that the work will end and that consideration has been given to what might follow. This is a matter of integrity in relation to the participants and those who might be employed as a result of the project. Participants and staff should be informed and supported into further opportunities, according to their individual hopes and aspirations.
- opportunities for further funding and support may be available if particular outcomes are achieved. For example, a programme which is piloted and then gains accreditation may be eligible for mainstream funding once the accreditation is in place. Planning for this eventuality from the beginning should inform the exit plans.
- the work may be designed to demonstrate to one or other service provider that a need exists and can be met. The service provider may be encouraged, during the delivery of the project, to support it.
- a partnership may be formed around a project which, as the project develops, may lead to different strands of activity which the partners are able to fund. This possibility needs to be considered at the beginning so that the right partners and allies are brought into the project.
- new funding opportunities may be on the horizon, such as European Social Funds (ESF) or Single Regeneration Budget (SRB) and a project may be planned with a view to accessing these funding streams. Whilst it is always inadvisable to follow funds rather than needs and ideas, planning should take account of future funding opportunities.

Dissemination forms an important part of the exit strategy by informing the potential funders and decision-makers about the future of the project. It is also a vital part of any initiative that other people in the field are offered the opportunity to learn from what has been organised and experienced, as well as from the outcomes. This helps the capacity of the sector to grow and encourages the sense of there being a community of learning and development amongst other providers and practitioners. Dissemination should be planned at the outset and carried out during the life of the project, in incremental ways, following celebrations of achievement and reviews or evaluation activities as well as at the end. (See *Conclusions and Dissemination*, page 33)

12 Conclusions and dissemination

The conclusions of a project can be broken into several parts:

- Evaluation of the whole project
- The final report
- Dissemination of the outcomes

Evaluation   Data which has been gathered during the project should also inform the final evaluation which could include such questions as:

- Were the aims and objectives met? If yes, list them; if not say why.
- Were the outcomes achieved? If yes, list them; if not say why.
- Was the planned budget spent? Did this present reasonable value for money and therefore indicate that it could be replicated?
- Were any unplanned or surprising outcomes achieved? If yes, list them.
- What processes, methods and approaches seemed to work most effectively?
- What were the greatest challenges of the project?
- How were they addressed?
- How might they have been addressed differently?
- What benefits were identified by and for participants, practitioners, providers, the partners and the wider community?
- Are there recommendations to be mad? To whom should they be addressed?
- What is going to happen next?

The final report should be written for the project sponsors. Other interested audiences will also want copies of the report, so multiple copies should be produced. The report should be built around the evaluation questions although many project sponsors set out their own requirements. Adding information about the stages, processes and the impact of quality assurance mechanisms will serve to support the description of what the project has done. The analysis of what has worked or not worked is helpful in encouraging the project to change future practices and in informing and changing the work of wider audiences. Recommendations are useful to sponsors as they help them to identify what kinds of activities they might fund next.

Enclosing quotes and feedback from those involved illustrates and illuminates the report. They also give immediate insight into the impact of the project upon people's lives and demonstrate the changes the project has initiated.

Photographs, videos, audio-tapes and examples of materials generated can also help to illuminate the final report. The trick is not to overwhelm the sponsor with so much information that s/he is disinclined to read it!

Dissemination of the final report should be considered carefully. A summary of the report might be produced, highlighting the main outcomes and achievements of the project, which can be sent to interested groups and organisations or distributed around the community. The production of the report might well coincide with a celebration event. If it doesn't, a final gathering of those most closely involved in the work should be considered. If the organisation has access to a web-site, the report can be published on it to reach a wider audience. The report should be available to key organisations including:

- project participants
- project sponsors
- all members of the management group
- all members of the steering group
- statutory organisations who may be interested in the outcomes, such as local authority departments and the Local Learning and Skills Council
- professional networks linked to aspects of the project
- local politicians.

Those who have been most closely involved in the project, including the participants, should be informed about the dissemination processes and about what is likely to happen after the end of the project. This is courteous and helps people to feel included through an understanding of the limitations of project work alongside an awareness of what might come next.

Sending press releases about the outcomes of the project and what is likely to happen next also helps in the dissemination process by raising the profile of the work and those involved.

NICK HAYES

13 Check it out

Good practice

- Starts with reflection on and analysis of the successful bid for project funding and the needs analysis on which it was based
- Reflects on the needs of the likely participants, the organisational context and the wider community context
- Bases planning on the aims of the project and the objectives designed to achieve the aims, following the above reflections
- Has a clear focus on the planned outcomes of the project and the opportunities to identify unanticipated outcomes
- Identifies the roles and responsibilities of the staff involved, whether they are part- or full-time, so that the project is managed and delivered successfully
- Differentiates between people who will be active partners and those who are allies or part of wider networks which will assist the success of the project
- Forms management and/or steering groups to support and assist in optimising the outcomes of the project
- Recognises the stages of the project, including its exit
- Develops a work-plan with the partners which is designed to plan, deliver, monitor, evaluate and disseminate the project
- Engages staff who are aware of the project parameters, its aims and objectives and their roles in achieving the outcomes; who are sensitive to the participants and who adopt an empowering, participatory approach to the development of the project
- Promotes equality of opportunity in all its practices, curriculum and materials by adopting open and well-communicated policies in relation to discrimination by gender, faith, race, sexuality and ability
- Manages staff by offering clear action planning, review and support in relation to achieving goals, work-load and health and safety
- Plans monitoring, review and evaluation of activities by participants, providers and partners, including responsible financial monitoring
- Reports regularly to project management and steering groups as well as the sponsors
- Disseminates the work and outcomes of the project at planned stages

- Celebrates the work and outcomes of the project, with all of those involved, at planned stages, in a variety of ways
- Supports the participants into further opportunities, according to their individual aims and aspirations
- Leaves the project in a planned way by accessing further developmental funding, embedding work into mainstream provision or supporting strands of activity with partners
- Produces a final report which is based upon the monitoring, review and evaluation data gathered during the life of the project
- Disseminates it to all those involved and makes it available to wider, interested audiences, to inform good practice and future development.

Challenges

- Projects are always risky as they try out new and different ways of working. This is a challenge for those who manage the project, the participants and the partners. It is also a difficulty for organisations which host projects as all parties feel their reputation can rest on the outcomes of the project.
- Projects can be marginalised from the mainstream of an organisation. They are often perceived as nothing to do with the central business.
- Short-term funding is always a challenge; it needs to be spent within a specified time and leaves the work developed without an obvious funding stream.
- Participants can feel sceptical about projects which come and go; many have seen such approaches before.
- Project staff are often part-time or temporary appointments.

Trouble-shooting

- By conducting a risk assessment at the beginning, a project can identify potential difficulties and highlight contingency plans. A supportive and pragmatic approach to project management can assist in promoting a no-blame culture. A sense of humour helps!
- Positive public relations strategies help projects in their relationships with participants, the community, the hosting organisation and their sponsors. Such approaches can also assist future funding.
- Projects need to consider how they relate to their wider organisation and plan internal communication and dissemination activities to help keep colleagues informed.

- Exit funding planning is a high priority and can involve looking at different sources of funds for continuing different parts of a project.
- Being honest and open about the purpose, timescale and the likely exit scenario of a project can help participants see that the project has genuine intentions.
- Deploying permanent staff to project work and substituting temporary staff to cover their time can help in diverting skills and experience whilst also offering developmental opportunities to less experienced colleagues.
- Project staff need to be included in development and training activities which support their work in the project but which also help to create routes for wider professional advancement.

Glossary

Accountability is the term used to describe the ways in which projects must be responsible in handling funds and reporting on their activities to the people they serve and the sponsors who support their work.

ACLF is the Adult and Community Learning Fund. This is the Government's innovation fund supporting projects which seek to develop new and interesting ways of reaching and teaching people who are not traditionally found in adult learning activities. It is an action research fund which aims to identify what works in widening participation.

Action-plans are the documents which individuals make to ensure that they work towards the work-plan goals and targets. They record actions, dates and who will carry them out and are used in reviews with line managers to monitor progress. They can change in the light of developments.

Allies and networks are the organisations which may assist a project from time to time, may be asked to contribute through service agreements or contracts or who are interested in some of the outcomes or spin-offs of the project. They may refer or receive participants or provide a wider network of support or information. They are less directly involved than project partners.

Capital is the funding used to purchase one-off items such as large pieces of equipment, buildings or vehicles. Capital can be described as having a lower limit e.g. items costing over £1,000.

Evaluation asks wide questions about whether the project is achieving what it set out to do, if changes are being experienced as anticipated, if the impact of the work is being felt amongst participants, the organisation and partners. Evaluation ensures that the project is examined in the light of the wider context of partnerships and the community it is serving as well as for the individuals involved. Evaluation is informed by the monitoring and review processes. It can be carried out within the project or by an appointed external evaluator.

Exit strategy is the plan which is made at the beginning of a project, to manage the end of the project in ways that are designed to sustain and continue the successful and developmental aspects of the work initiated.

Management group meets regularly to monitor the progress of a project and make decisions about changes which may need to be implemented. It has responsibility for ensuring the success of the project and supports the project manager and co-ordinator to achieve the outcomes declared. The membership is drawn from the partners and those responsible for handling the funds of the project.

Monitoring is the process of checking against plans, milestones, goals and targets that the project is progressing towards the planned outcomes.

Partners are the organisations which are prepared to commit resources to a project and which will benefit from the outcomes of the work. Partners have something to give and to gain from being involved in a project.

Revenue is the funding used to run activities, purchase consumable and small items of equipment, and pay staff and accommodation costs.

Review is conducted with individuals or groups, staff or participants in a formative way, to discover how they feel about their involvement in the project, what they are learning or developing, what is going well and what could be changed or improved.

SMART is the acronym used to describe the process of planning and target-setting. S = Specific, M = Measurable, A = Achievable, R = Relevant, T = Time-bound.

Steering group meets less regularly than the management group and has membership drawn from the wider community and the allies and networks of the project. It makes recommendations to the project and receives information on progress as well as feeds back information on the effectiveness of the work. Members contribute to the wider evaluation questions and can help in sustaining strands of work after the project is over.

Sustainability plans are similar to exit plans in that they address issues of maintaining some, if not all, of the work started on a project. Using other strands of funding, asking partners to take on some aspects of development and absorbing some work into existing programmes are approaches which can be considered.

Work-plans are the recorded and shared documents which lay out how the project will work towards achieving its goals and targets. They record milestones, meetings and approximate dates of activities designed to keep the project progressing towards its outcomes. Work-plans can be monitored by management groups and steering groups and amended in the light of successes and challenges.

Further reading

Evaluation of the Adult and Community Learning Fund (2001) DfES, Sheffield

Lessons from the Community (ACLF) (2001) NIACE, Leicester

Management Development Super Series NEBS, (1997) Pergamon Open Learning, Oxford

Project Management, The Institute of Management (1997) Pergamon Open Learning, Oxford

Voices of Practitioners: Good Practice in Adult and Community Learning, Jan Eldred, NIACE/DfES, Leicester

Useful contacts and networks

Acre (Action with Communities in Rural England)
Somerford Court
Somerford Road
Cirencester GL17 1TW
Tel: 01285 53477
Email: acre@acre.org.uk
Website: www.acre.org.uk

CDF (Community Development Foundation)
60 Highbury Grove
London N5 2AG
Tel: 020 7226 5375
Email: admin@cdf.org.uk
Website: www.cdf.org.uk

CEDC (Community Education Development Centre)
Unit C1
Grovelands Court
Grovelands Estate
Longford Road
Exhall
Coventry CV7 9NE
Tel: 024 7658 8440
Email: info@cedc.org.uk
Website: www.cedc.org.uk

Community Matters
12-20 Baron Street
London N1 9LL
Tel: 020 7837 7887
Email: communitymatters@communitymatters.org.uk
Website: www.communitymatters.org.uk